MW00917253

IF FOUND PLEASE RETURN TO:

_____

_____

_____

EMAIL: _____

REWARD: _____

2022 - 2023 - 2024

January 2022

Sunday	Monday	Tuesday	Wednesday
2	3	4	5
9	10	11	12
16	17	18	19
23 30	24 31	25	26

"The pessimist sees difficulty in every opportunity. The optimist sees the opportunity in every difficulty." -Winston Churchill

Thursday	Friday	Saturday
		1
6	7	8
13	14	15
20	21	22
27	28	29

Notes

_____
_____
_____
_____
_____
_____
_____
_____
_____
_____
_____
_____
_____
_____
_____
_____
_____
_____
_____
_____
_____
_____

February 2022

Sunday	Monday	Tuesday	Wednesday
		1	2
6	7	8	9
13	14	15	16
20	21	22	23
27	28		

"It's not whether you get knocked down, it's whether you get up."
-Vince Lombardi

Thursday 3	Friday 4	Saturday 5	Notes
10	11	12	
17	18	19	
24	25	26	

March 2022

Sunday	Monday	Tuesday	Wednesday
		1	2
6	7	8	9
13	14	15	16
20	21	22	23
27	28	29	30

"We may encounter many defeats but we must not be defeated."
-Maya Angelou

Thursday 3	Friday 4	Saturday 5
10	11	12
17	18	19
24	25	26
31		

Notes

_____
_____
_____
_____
_____
_____
_____
_____
_____
_____
_____
_____
_____
_____
_____
_____
_____
_____
_____
_____
_____
_____
_____
_____
_____
_____
_____
_____

April 2022

Sunday	Monday	Tuesday	Wednesday
3	4	5	6
10	11	12	13
17	18	19	20
24	25	26	27

"The only limit to our realization of tomorrow will be our doubts of today." -Franklin D. Roosevelt

Thursday	Friday	Saturday	Notes
	1	2	
7	8	9	
14	15	16	
21	22	23	
28	29	30	

May 2022

Sunday	Monday	Tuesday	Wednesday
1	2	3	4
8	9	10	11
15	16	17	18
22	23	24	25
29	30	31	

"The world breaks everyone, and afterward, some are strong at the broken places." - Ernest Hemingway

Thursday 5	Friday 6	Saturday 7	Notes
12	13	14	
19	20	21	
26	27	28	

June 2022

Sunday	Monday	Tuesday	Wednesday 1
5	6	7	8
12	13	14	15
19	20	21	22
26	27	28	29

"A truly strong person does not need the approval of others any more than a lion needs the approval of sheep." -Vernon Howard

Thursday 2	Friday 3	Saturday 4
9	10	11
16	17	18
23	24	25
30		

Notes

July 2022

Sunday	Monday	Tuesday	Wednesday
3	4	5	6
10	11	12	13
17	18	19	20
24 31	25	26	27

"Tough times never last, but tough people do." -Robert H. Schuller

Thursday	Friday	Saturday	Notes
	1	2	
7	8	9	
14	15	16	
21	22	23	
28	29	30	

August 2022

Sunday	Monday	Tuesday	Wednesday
	1	2	3
7	8	9	10
14	15	16	17
21	22	23	24
28	29	30	31

"Winning doesn't always mean being first. Winning means you're doing better than you've ever done before." -Bonnie Blair

Thursday 4	Friday 5	Saturday 6	Notes
11	12	13	
18	19	20	
25	26	27	

September 2022

Sunday	Monday	Tuesday	Wednesday
4	5	6	7
11	12	13	14
18	19	20	21
25	26	27	28

"There are always new, grander challenges to confront, and a true winner will embrace each one." -Mia Hamm

Thursday 1	Friday 2	Saturday 3
8	9	10
15	16	17
22	23	24
29	30	

Notes

_____
_____
_____
_____
_____
_____
_____
_____
_____
_____
_____
_____
_____
_____
_____
_____
_____
_____
_____
_____
_____
_____
_____

October 2022

Sunday	Monday	Tuesday	Wednesday
2	3	4	5
9	10	11	12
16	17	18	19
23 30	24 31	25	26

"Winning isn't everything, but wanting it is." - Arnold Palmer

Thursday	Friday	Saturday
		1
6	7	8
13	14	15
20	21	22
27	28	29

Notes

_____
_____
_____
_____
_____
_____
_____
_____
_____
_____
_____
_____
_____
_____
_____
_____
_____
_____
_____
_____
_____
_____
_____
_____

November 2022

Sunday	Monday	Tuesday	Wednesday
		1	2
6	7	8	9
13	14	15	16
20	21	22	23
27	28	29	30

"The bamboo that bends is stronger than the oak that resists." -Japanese Proverb

Thursday 3	Friday 4	Saturday 5	Notes
10	11	12	
17	18	19	
24	25	26	

December 2022

Sunday	Monday	Tuesday	Wednesday
4	5	6	7
11	12	13	14
18	19	20	21
25	26	27	28

"Be yourself; everyone else is already taken." - Oscar Wilde

Thursday	Friday	Saturday	Notes
1	2	3	
8	9	10	
15	16	17	
22	23	24	
29	30	31	

January *2023*

Sunday	Monday	Tuesday	Wednesday
1	2	3	4
8	9	10	11
15	16	17	18
22	23	24	25
29	30	31	

"Never be ashamed! There's some who will hold it against you, but they are not worth bothering with." - J.K, Rowling

Thursday 5	Friday 6	Saturday 7	Notes
12	13	14	
19	20	21	
26	27	28	

February 2023

Sunday	Monday	Tuesday	Wednesday
			1
5	6	7	8
12	13	14	15
19	20	21	22
26	27	28	

"Be undeniably good. No marketing effort or social media buzzword can be a substitute for that." - Anthony Volodkin

Thursday 2	Friday 3	Saturday 4	Notes
9	10	11	
16	17	18	
23	24	25	

March 2023

Sunday	Monday	Tuesday	Wednesday
			1
5	6	7	8
12	13	14	15
19	20	21	22
26	27	28	29

"Optimism is the faith that leads to achievement. Nothing can be done without hope and confidence." - Helen Keller

Thursday 2	Friday 3	Saturday 4	Notes
9	10	11	
16	17	18	
23	24	25	
30	31		

April 2023

Sunday	Monday	Tuesday	Wednesday
2	3	4	5
9	10	11	12
16	17	18	19
23 30	24	25	26

"Chase the vision, not the money. The money will end up following you." - Tony Hsieh

Thursday	Friday	Saturday
		1
6	7	8
13	14	15
20	21	22
27	28	29

Notes

_____
_____
_____
_____
_____
_____
_____
_____
_____
_____
_____
_____
_____
_____
_____
_____
_____
_____
_____
_____
_____
_____
_____
_____
_____

May 2023

Sunday	Monday	Tuesday	Wednesday
	1	2	3
7	8	9	10
14	15	16	17
21	22	23	24
28	29	30	31

"Don't try to be original, just try to be good." -Paul Rand

Thursday 4	Friday 5	Saturday 6	Notes
11	12	13	
18	19	20	
25	26	27	

June 2023

Sunday	Monday	Tuesday	Wednesday
4	5	6	7
11	12	13	14
18	19	20	21
25	26	27	28

"The only thing worse than starting something and failing ... is not starting something." -Seth Godin

Thursday 1	Friday 2	Saturday 3	Notes
8	9	10	
15	16	17	
22	23	24	
29	30		

July 2023

Sunday	Monday	Tuesday	Wednesday
2	3	4	5
9	10	11	12
16	17	18	19
23	24	25	26
30	31		

"When I'm old and dying, I plan to look back on my life and say, 'Wow, that was an adventure,' not, 'Wow, I sure felt safe." -Tom Preston-Werner

Thursday	Friday	Saturday	Notes
		1	
6	7	8	
13	14	15	
20	21	22	
27	28	29	

August 2023

Sunday	Monday	Tuesday	Wednesday
		1	2
6	7	8	9
13	14	15	16
20	21	22	23
27	28	29	30

"What do you need to start a business? Three simple things: Know your product better than anyone. Know your customer, and have a burning desire to succeed." -Dave Thomas

Thursday 3	Friday 4	Saturday 5	Notes
10	11	12	
17	18	19	
24	25	26	
31			

September 2023

Sunday	Monday	Tuesday	Wednesday
3	4	5	6
10	11	12	13
17	18	19	20
24	25	26	27

"Fearlessness is like a muscle. I know from my own life that the more I exercise it the more natural it becomes to not let my fears run me." -Arianna Huffington

Thursday	Friday	Saturday
	1	2
7	8	9
14	15	16
21	22	23
28	29	30

Notes

_____
_____
_____
_____
_____
_____
_____
_____
_____
_____
_____
_____
_____
_____
_____
_____
_____
_____
_____
_____
_____
_____
_____
_____
_____
_____

October   2023

Sunday	Monday	Tuesday	Wednesday
1	2	3	4
8	9	10	11
15	16	17	18
22	23	24	25
29	30	31	

"Small business isn't for the faint of heart. It's for the brave, the patient, and the persistent. It's for the overcomer." -Unknown

Thursday 5	Friday 6	Saturday 7	Notes
12	13	14	
19	20	21	
26	27	28	

November $\quad$ 2023

Sunday	Monday	Tuesday	Wednesday
			1
5	6	7	8
12	13	14	15
19	20	21	22
26	27	28	29

"I can't imagine a person becoming a success who doesn't give this game of life everything he's got." -Walter Cronkite

Thursday 2	Friday 3	Saturday 4	Notes
9	10	11	
16	17	18	
23	24	25	
30			

December 2023

Sunday	Monday	Tuesday	Wednesday
3	4	5	6
10	11	12	13
17	18	19	20
24 31	25	26	27

"I don't focus on what I'm up against. I focus on my goals and I try to ignore the rest." -Venus Williams

Thursday	Friday	Saturday
	1	2
7	8	9
14	15	16
21	22	23
28	29	30

Notes

January 2024

Sunday	Monday	Tuesday	Wednesday
	1	2	3
7	8	9	10
14	15	16	17
21	22	23	24
28	29	30	31

"Success is liking yourself, liking what you do, and liking how you do it." -Maya Angelou

Thursday 4	Friday 5	Saturday 6	Notes
11	12	13	
18	19	20	
25	26	27	

February 2024

Sunday	Monday	Tuesday	Wednesday
4	5	6	7
11	12	13	14
18	19	20	21
25	26	27	28

"I knew that if I failed I wouldn't regret that, but I knew the one thing I might regret is not trying." -Jeff Bezos

Thursday 1	Friday 2	Saturday 3	Notes
8	9	10	
15	16	17	
22	23	24	
29			

March

2024

Sunday	Monday	Tuesday	Wednesday
3	4	5	6
10	11	12	13
17	18	19	20
24	25	26	27
31			

"Remember to celebrate milestones as you prepare for the road ahead." -Nelson Mandela

Thursday	Friday	Saturday
	1	2
7	8	9
14	15	16
21	22	23
28	29	30

Notes

April 2024

Sunday	Monday	Tuesday	Wednesday
	1	2	3
7	8	9	10
14	15	16	17
21	22	23	24
28	29	30	

"The only limit to our realization of tomorrow will be our doubts of today." -Franklin D. Roosevelt

Thursday 4	Friday 5	Saturday 6	Notes
11	12	13	
18	19	20	
25	26	27	

May 2024

Sunday	Monday	Tuesday	Wednesday
			1
5	6	7	8
12	13	14	15
19	20	21	22
26	27	28	29

"The world breaks everyone, and afterward, some are strong at the broken places." - Ernest Hemingway

Thursday 2	Friday 3	Saturday 4	Notes
9	10	11	
16	17	18	
23	24	25	
30	31		

June 2024

Sunday	Monday	Tuesday	Wednesday
2	3	4	5
9	10	11	12
16	17	18	19
23 30	24	25	26

"A truly strong person does not need the approval of others any more than a lion needs the approval of sheep." -Vernon Howard

Thursday	Friday	Saturday
		1
6	7	8
13	14	15
20	21	22
27	28	29

Notes

July 2024

Sunday	Monday	Tuesday	Wednesday
	1	2	3
7	8	9	10
14	15	16	17
21	22	23	24
28	29	30	31

"Tough times never last, but tough people do." -Robert H. Schuller

Thursday 4	Friday 5	Saturday 6	Notes
11	12	13	
18	19	20	
25	26	27	

August 2024

Sunday	Monday	Tuesday	Wednesday
4	5	6	7
11	12	13	14
18	19	20	21
25	26	27	28

"Winning doesn't always mean being first. Winning means you're doing better than you've ever done before." -Bonnie Blair

Thursday 1	Friday 2	Saturday 3
8	9	10
15	16	17
22	23	24
29	30	31

Notes

September 2024

Sunday	Monday	Tuesday	Wednesday
1	2	3	4
8	9	10	11
15	16	17	18
22	23	24	25
29	30		

"There are always new, grander challenges to confront, and a true winner will embrace each one." -Mia Hamm

Thursday 5	Friday 6	Saturday 7
12	13	14
19	20	21
26	27	28

Notes

_____
_____
_____
_____
_____
_____
_____
_____
_____
_____
_____
_____
_____
_____
_____
_____
_____
_____
_____
_____
_____
_____
_____
_____
_____
_____

October

2024

Sunday	Monday	Tuesday	Wednesday
		1	2
6	7	8	9
13	14	15	16
20	21	22	23
27	28	29	30

"Winning isn't everything, but wanting it is." -Arnold Palmer

Thursday 3	Friday 4	Saturday 5	Notes
10	11	12	
17	18	19	
24	25	26	
31			

November 2024

Sunday	Monday	Tuesday	Wednesday
3	4	5	6
10	11	12	13
17	18	19	20
24	25	26	27

"The bamboo that bends is stronger than the oak that resists." -Japanese Proverb

Thursday	Friday	Saturday	Notes
	1	2	_____
			_____
			_____
			_____
7	8	9	_____
			_____
			_____
			_____
			_____
14	15	16	_____
			_____
			_____
			_____
			_____
21	22	23	_____
			_____
			_____
			_____
28	29	30	_____
			_____
			_____
			_____

December 2024

Sunday	Monday	Tuesday	Wednesday
1	2	3	4
8	9	10	11
15	16	17	18
22	23	24	25
29	30	31	

"Be yourself; everyone else is already taken." - Oscar Wilde

Thursday 5	Friday 6	Saturday 7	Notes
12	13	14	
19	20	21	
26	27	28	

SCAN ME

Made in the USA
Monee, IL
10 May 2022

96160178R00083